AF598980

REPORTERS
ON 9/11
15
POLICE
BY JANIE HAVEMEYER
childsworld.com

Published by The Child's World®
800-599-READ • www.childsworld.com

Photography Credits
Photographs ©: Boudicon One/AP Images, cover, 1; Walter Cicchetti/Shutterstock Images, 5; Andrew Harnik/AP Images, 6; National Institute of Standards and Technology, 8; Anthony Correia/Shutterstock Images, 10; Shutterstock Images, 11; Bob Riha, Jr./Archive Photos/Getty Images, 12; David Handschuh/KRT/Abaca Press/Alamy, 15; Carol M. Highsmith/Library of Congress, 16, 28; Hubert Boesl/picture-alliance/dpa/AP Images, 19; National Archives/DVIDS, 20; Kenneth Lambert/AP Images, 21; Petty Officer 1st Class Mark D. Faram/US Navy/US Department of Defense, 22; Red Line Editorial, 24; Mark Faram/USNR/US Navy Archives/Naval History and Heritage Command, 25; Gary Blakeley/Shutterstock Images, 26

ISBN Information
9781503889132 (Reinforced Library Binding)
9781503890879 (Portable Document Format)
9781503892118 (Online Multi-user eBook)
9781503893351 (Electronic Publication)

LCCN 2023950403

Printed in the United States of America

ABOUT THE AUTHOR

Janie Havemeyer is an author of many books for young readers. Havemeyer lives in San Francisco, California, but grew up in New York City. She knew many people in New York City personally affected by the September 11 attacks. When Janie is not writing, she likes to read, take hikes, spend time with her family, and travel.

CONTENTS

FAST FACTS

- On September 11, 2001, **terrorists** attacked the United States. They **hijacked** four airplanes and planned to crash them into important buildings.
- Two planes hit the Twin Towers of the World Trade Center in New York City. One plane crashed into the Pentagon near Washington, DC. The fourth plane crashed into a field near Shanksville, Pennsylvania.
- Jon Hilsenrath worked for the *Wall Street Journal* on September 11. His stories were published on the front page of the September 12 edition of the newspaper.
- David Handschuh was injured while taking photos of the September 11 attacks.
- Thomas Franklin took a photo that became one of the most well-known from the September 11 attacks.
- Sandra Jontz was a reporter working at the Pentagon during the September 11 attacks. She worked to give a voice to victims from the Pentagon.
- Jon Meyer was the first journalist at the Flight 93 crash site.

The September 11 attacks made headlines around the world.

Si segue la pista del terrorista Osama Bin Laden
Glauco Maggi
1:58PM Smoke engulfs the south tower of the World Trade Center after the first Boeing slams into it
2.05PM A second jet with 64 aboard approaches the twin towers, where 25,000 people worked
THE MIRROR, Wednesday, September 12, 2001
THE Mirror
Wednesday September 12 2001
275 ptas
PRINTED TODAY IN SPAIN, THE CANARIES & MAJORCA
By Joseph Fitchett
International Herald Tribune

CHAPTER ONE

JON HILSENRATH

Jon Hilsenrath was sitting in the *Wall Street Journal*'s newsroom when another reporter started screaming. Hilsenrath dashed to the window. His office was right across the street from the World Trade Center in New York City. There were flames pouring out of the North Tower's upper floors. It was 8:47 a.m. on September 11, 2001.

Hilsenrath was a reporter for the *Journal*. He usually reported on issues about the **economy**. But on this day, a major event was happening right next door. He had to find out what was going on. He grabbed his notebook and ran. He was determined to interview **eyewitnesses** who might explain what they had seen.

When Hilsenrath reached the street, he saw smoking **debris** scattered all over. People were shouting and screaming.

◄ **Today, Jon Hilsenrath is an editor and senior writer at the *Wall Street Journal*.**

Sirens blared. He began to describe the sights and sounds in his notebook. His hand shook as he wrote. Hilsenrath stood near 3 World Trade Center, a hotel. But a police officer yelled at him to leave the area. Hilsenrath was not sure what to do.

WALL STREET JOURNAL *OFFICE*

The *Wall Street Journal*'s office was in the World Financial Center near the World Trade Center.

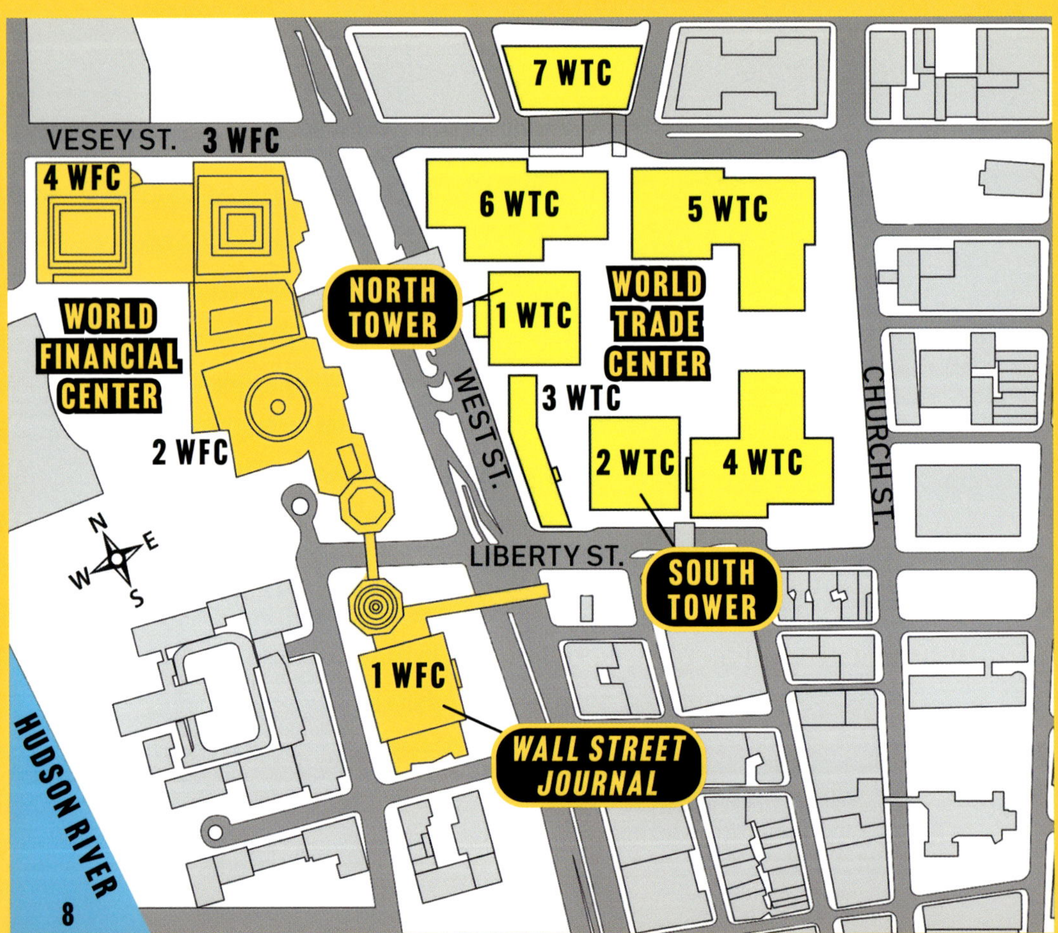

He did not want to be in the way, but he felt it was his duty as a journalist to stay nearby. He began slowly walking away, still taking notes.

Then Hilsenrath heard the roar of an airplane. It was flying low in the sky. Hilsenrath could make out the blue belly of the plane. He started running. Then there was a loud *boom*. The plane had crashed into the South Tower of the World Trade Center. Hilsenrath realized the first explosion had not been an accident. The city was under attack. Hilsenrath and hundreds of people around him stared up at the tower. He could see a hole in the South Tower where clouds of paper swirled out.

About an hour later, Hilsenrath heard another roar. He thought it might be another plane. He did not want to get hurt, so he ran west toward the Hudson River. "If I have to, I'll jump in the river," he thought. He did not realize the sound was the South Tower collapsing. A white cloud of dust roared toward him. Flakes of ash and dust spread over him like a blanket. He covered his mouth with his shirt. After the dust settled, Hilsenrath thought about what to do next. He tried calling his wife as he searched for a route away from the World Trade Center. He knew she was worried about him. But the call did not go through. Cell phone networks were overwhelmed with calls, and many calls did not connect. But Hilsenrath was able to get in touch with his brother.

Dust from the collapse of the Twin Towers spread for miles.

Hilsenrath asked him to call his wife and parents to let them know he was alive.

Hilsenrath spent the rest of the day interviewing survivors. It was easy to recognize people who had been there. He just looked for people covered in white dust. Later that day, he called the *Wall Street Journal*'s office in Dallas, Texas, to share his notes. His New York office had been badly damaged.

Hilsenrath's reporting made it into the *Wall Street Journal*'s front-page articles on September 12. He had watched history unfold. His story helped explain what had happened.

Jon Hilsenrath was part of a team at the *Wall Street Journal* that won a Pulitzer Prize, the highest honor in news coverage, for their reporting on 9/11.

1155
AVENUE
OF THE
AMERICAS
THE
WALL
STREET
JOURNAL

CHAPTER TWO

DAVID HANDSCHUH

David Handschuh was sitting in bumper-to-bumper traffic on September 11, 2001, when he noticed a large cloud of smoke. It was rising up from the World Trade Center. Handschuh was a staff photographer for the *New York Daily News*. But this morning, he was heading to teach a class at New York University.

David Handschuh returned to the site of the World Trade Center attacks in December of 2001.

He thought a pilot might have flown a small plane into the building by accident. He called his newsroom and asked if they wanted him to go down there. His boss told him to go quickly.

Handschuh arrived at the World Trade Center at 8:53 a.m. It was quiet on the street, but flames poured out of the North Tower. First responders were arriving on the scene. West Street was littered with papers, broken glass, and airplane parts. People were running. Women carried their high heels so they could run faster. Some people held serving trays over their heads to protect themselves from falling debris. Cars and vans were burning. Handschuh aimed his camera lens at the top of the Twin Towers. He snapped photo after photo. Then he heard a high-pitched roar and the South Tower exploded. It had been hit by another plane.

Handschuh kept taking photos until a loud bang made him pause. The ground shook as the South Tower began to crumble. Handschuh's instincts told him to run. He rounded the corner at Liberty Street when a wave of hot gravel, glass, cement, and metal sent him flying into the air. He landed under a car, one block from where he had been. A cloud of debris made it hard to breathe. Handschuh had lost his cell phone, **pager**, and glasses, but he still held onto his cameras.

Firefighters dug him out. "Don't worry, brother. We'll get you out," they told him. First responders carried Handschuh to a nearby **delicatessen**. His leg was shattered and his pants were torn. The deli was supposed to be a temporary safe place to hide. But when the North Tower collapsed at 10:28 a.m., the front of the deli was crushed, too. Handschuh was trapped once again. He looked around and recognized Todd Maisel, a coworker from the *Daily News*, trapped with him. Handschuh handed Maisel his cameras to take into the office. If Handschuh survived, he would be going to the hospital instead of the newsroom.

The next day, one of Handschuh's photos was printed in the *Daily News*. It was a picture of the South Tower just seconds after the plane hit. After a long and difficult recovery period, Handschuh returned to work. He was haunted by what he had seen that day. "The people behind the photographs, who stood there and took them—when the sensible thing would be to run like [crazy]—put themselves at personal risk because they considered it more important to inform the world about what happened," he said.

Handschuh has stayed in touch with the men who carried him to safety. "I regularly meet with the rescuers, and we hug and cry," Handschuh said. "There is nothing I can do to adequately say 'Thank you' for allowing me to live."

Handschuh's famous photo captured the South Tower just after the plane hit.

CHAPTER THREE

THOMAS FRANKLIN

Thomas Franklin worked in the photo department of the New Jersey newspaper *The Record*. At 9 a.m. on September 11, 2001, Franklin was in the office earlier than usual. He was talking to his editor about an assignment. Suddenly, another editor rushed in to say a plane had crashed into the World Trade Center. Franklin grabbed his camera and ran outside. He made his way to the New Jersey waterfront. Huge plumes of smoke rose into the blue sky from the World Trade Center, just half a mile (.8 km) across the Hudson River. Franklin took photos. Soon, rescue boats carrying injured people came from across the river. The injured were covered in white dust. Franklin took photos of firefighters being carried away in stretchers. It was a difficult place to take pictures. People were running everywhere.

The Twin Towers were just across the Hudson River from New Jersey.

Police officers tried to clear people out of the area, including Franklin. "Almost got arrested a couple times," he later said in an interview. Franklin managed to call his office. They told him to get to Manhattan if he could. Franklin ran into John Wheeler, another photographer who sometimes worked for *The Record*. Wheeler knew a police official. Franklin and Wheeler were able to get a ride across the river on a police tugboat.

On the Manhattan side of the river, the boat captain handed Franklin and Wheeler bottled water and masks. He told them to be careful. The photographers made their way toward the ruins of the Twin Towers. Everything was covered in white dust. Franklin could see shards of metal everywhere. He walked around shooting photos. There were first responders looking for survivors. Firefighters were putting out flames from the smoking wreckage. Franklin tried to focus on taking pictures. But it was hard not to think about his friends and family who worked in this area. He hoped they were not hurt.

Around 4:45 p.m., firefighters began to **evacuate** the area. Another building, 7 World Trade Center, was about to collapse. Franklin followed the firefighters to a first aid station. Hundreds of first responders were there. Everyone was quiet with their heads down. It was like being at a funeral.

September 11, 2001, was the largest water evacuation in history. Approximately 500,000 people were rescued by boat from the area near the World Trade Center.

Franklin's camera was running low on memory. He had to delete images to be able to take more. "While I was doing this, I saw these three firemen fumbling with the flag, getting ready to raise it," he said. "It didn't immediately register to me what they were about to do, but I knew it seemed significant." Franklin got into position and changed his lens. He shot many photos of the firefighters raising the flag.

The Battle of Iwo Jima was an important World War II battle.

Franklin went back to New Jersey on another police boat. He set up his laptop in a nearby hotel to look at all his photos. The shot of the firemen raising the flag reminded him of a famous World War II (1939–1945) photo. That photo was of soldiers raising an American flag on the Japanese island of Iwo Jima in 1945. The next day, Franklin's photo of the three firemen was published in *The Record*. It is called *Raising the Flag at Ground Zero*. Afterward, many news outlets asked to republish it. The photo went global.

▲ **Thomas Franklin's (right) famous photo was turned into a postage stamp. President George W. Bush (left) and the Postmaster General (center) revealed the stamp at a ceremony in March 2002.**

September 11 was the hardest day of Franklin's life as a photographer. But he is thankful his photo touched so many people. "Years later and I still get letters from people . . . [telling] me that the photograph makes them think of a lost loved one or reminds them of their patriotism or their faith in our country," Franklin said.

CHAPTER FOUR

SANDRA JONTZ

The Pentagon is the headquarters of the United States Defense Department near Washington, DC. On the morning of September 11, 2001, Pentagon employees ran through the halls. "Evacuate the building! There's been an explosion!" they shouted.

Sandra Jontz and other medical personnel at the Pentagon on 9/11 wore blue vests.

Sandra Jontz was at her desk at 9:37 a.m. when she felt a *thud* that shook the building. Jontz was a reporter for the *European and Pacific Stars and Stripes*. This was a military newspaper for members living overseas. Jontz wanted to find out what had happened. She grabbed her notebook, tape recorder, phone, and briefcase. Instead of evacuating the building, she headed to the central courtyard of the Pentagon.

Jontz was shocked when she reached the courtyard. She was also a trained **EMT**. She had been on the scene of accidents before. But she had never seen so many people with serious burns. Gray smoke billowed from the building. A plane had crashed into the west side of the Pentagon. Jontz wanted to find out more, but she put her reporter duties aside to help the wounded. Jontz asked a woman in a lab coat how she could help.

Jontz went to work helping to treat victims. Jontz helped insert an **IV** into a patient's arm. She cut open another patient's shirt to check for wounds. Then someone said, "Hurry up. Another plane inbound, another plane inbound. We've gotta get out of here!" Officials had learned that Flight 93 was heading toward Washington, DC. Some people thought it might be on its way to hit the Pentagon again. Jontz helped load patients into vehicles.

Then she fled to the front of the building. She could see where a plane had hit light poles in the street before striking the Pentagon. The poles lay like matchsticks across a field.

Doctors soon arrived and organized the medical workers and patients. Later that afternoon, Jontz began interviewing people. A former marine told her he had helped a woman crawl through a window. She had been badly burned. Jontz moved to a bus that was set up to give medical aid to firefighters battling the fires.

HOW THE NEWS AFFECTED PEOPLE

At least 80 million people were watching news coverage of the attacks on the evening of September 11, 2001. The Pew Research Center surveyed 1,200 Americans in the days after September 11 to see what effect the media coverage was having on people.

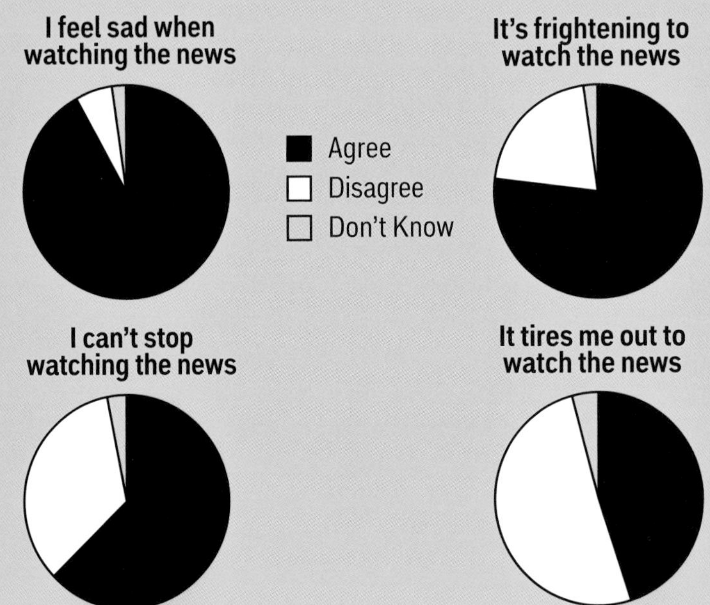

Plane parts and other debris were scattered in the fields near the Pentagon.

She helped treat them until 1:30 a.m., then went home for a few hours of sleep.

The next morning, Jontz went to a gas station near the Pentagon. Members of the media gathered there. She interviewed rescue teams and family members waiting for news about their loved ones. Jontz worked at the gas station for two days, taking notes and writing articles. Her laptop was trapped in her office, so she read her articles over the phone to her editor. Jontz's stories of the Pentagon attacks were published all over Europe and the Pacific. Jontz said, "I was proud to cover the Pentagon and the friends and families of the victims because other media were overlooking the Pentagon." Jontz worked to make sure people knew the 9/11 attacks affected more than just the World Trade Center.

CHAPTER FIVE

JON MEYER

On September 11, 2001, Jon Meyer was 24 years old. He worked as a reporter for WJAC, a television station in Johnstown, Pennsylvania. He had heard about the attacks in New York before coming to work. When he got to the newsroom, Meyer and his coworkers learned that a plane was missing.

◄ **Live trucks allow journalists to broadcast from the scene of breaking news events.**

Soon, calls began coming into the newsroom. Eyewitnesses reported a plane crash about 23 miles (37 km) away near the farming town of Shanksville, Pennsylvania. Meyer and photographer J. D. Kirkpatrick raced out of the newsroom. They jumped into their live truck and headed for Shanksville.

When they arrived, they parked the truck on a small hill. Kirkpatrick gathered his camera equipment while Meyer ran down to the field. He was looking for the plane. He thought he might need to help survivors of the crash. Meyer ran toward the smoke coming from the other end of the field. But when he reached the crash site, all he saw was a deep crater. The plane had hit so hard, the ground had swallowed it up. There were no recognizable plane parts, just a pit of burning debris. A strong smell of jet fuel filled the air as fires burned around the site.

Firefighters and state troopers had arrived on the scene, too. "What happened here?" Meyer asked. No one knew the answer. Meyer began to take notes describing the crash site. He knew he needed to remember the details. But soon, state troopers asked him to leave. They had stopped Kirkpatrick farther away. Officials did not want the media at the site. Meyer was the first reporter on the scene. He had been one of the few to get close to the site.

A national memorial honoring the victims onboard Flight 93 was built on the crash site near Shanksville, Pennsylvania.

Meyer and Kirkpatrick made their way back to the live truck. They began broadcasting. "The only way to describe this is haunting," Meyer reported.

Meyer continued following the September 11 story. United Airlines Flight 93 had been the fourth plane hijacked on September 11. The passengers had tried to take back the plane from the hijackers. It crashed into the field during the struggle. Flight 93 was likely heading for the White House or the US Capitol in Washington, DC. The passengers kept it from reaching its target. "It was the honor of my life to help share the story of the heroes on board Flight 93," Meyer said many years later.

THINK ABOUT IT

- What are ways reporters can stay safe while reporting in dangerous situations?
- Why do you think *Raising the Flag at Ground Zero* became one of the most famous 9/11 images?
- The world was a different place in 2001. Many people did not have cell phones, and there was no social media. How do you think reporting about 9/11 was different than reporting on disasters today?

GLOSSARY

debris (duh-BREE): Debris is made up of pieces of things that have been destroyed or broken down. New York City was covered in debris from the collapse of the Twin Towers.

delicatessen (deh-lih-kuh-TESS-sun): A delicatessen, or deli, is a store that sells ready-to-eat food such as cooked meats and salads. David Handschuh took cover in a delicatessen on 9/11.

economy (eh-KAH-nuh-mee): The economy is how a country uses money to create and divide goods between people. Jon Hilsenrath usually wrote about the economy for the *Wall Street Journal*.

EMT: An EMT (emergency medical technician) provides emergency medical care to people who are ill or injured away from a doctor's office or hospital. Sandra Jontz was a trained EMT.

evacuate (eh-VAK-yoo-ayt): To evacuate means to leave a place where one might be in danger. People were told to evacuate the Pentagon on the morning of September 11, 2001.

eyewitnesses (eye-WIT-nuss-es): Eyewitnesses have seen something happen and can give a firsthand description of it. Eyewitnesses described Flight 93's crash.

hijacked (HY-jakt): When something has been hijacked, it has been taken over by force. Four airplanes were hijacked on 9/11.

IV: An IV is a thin, bendable tube used to give medicine and fluids directly into a patient's veins. Sandra Jontz helped with IV insertion for victims at the Pentagon.

pager (PAY-jur): A pager is a device that vibrates or beeps when it receives a message. David Handschuh lost his pager on 9/11.

terrorists (TAYR-ur-ists): Terrorists are people who commit violent acts to make people feel fear or terror. On September 11, 2001, terrorists flew airplanes into buildings.

SELECTED BIBLIOGRAPHY

Bull, Chris and Sam Erman, editors. *At Ground Zero: Young Reporters Who Were There Tell Their Stories*. New York, NY: Thunder's Mouth Press, 2002.

PBS Digital Studios. "The Real Story Behind This Iconic 9/11 Photo." *PBS*, 6 Sept. 2022, www.pbs.org. Accessed 4 Jan. 2024.

Rotbart, Dean. *September Twelfth: An American Comeback Story*. Denver, CO: TJFR Press, 2021.

FIND OUT MORE

BOOKS

Forest, Christopher. *September 11th Attacks*. Minneapolis, MN: Jump!, 2021.

Rea, Amy C. *Citizen Heroes on 9/11*. Parker, CO: The Child's World, 2025.

Romero, Libby. *September 11*. Washington, DC: National Geographic, 2021.

WEBSITES

Visit our website for links about reporters on 9/11:
childsworld.com/links

Note to Parents, Caregivers, Teachers, and Librarians: We routinely verify our web links to make sure they are safe and active sites. So encourage your readers to check them out!

INDEX